Learn How To Argue In Your Next Negotiation

How To Develop The Skill Of Effective Arguing In A Negotiation In Order To Get The Best Possible Outcome

"Practical, proven techniques that will help you get the best deal possible out of your next negotiation"

Dr. Jim Anderson

Published by:
Blue Elephant Consulting
Tampa, Florida

Copyright © 2013 by Dr. Jim Anderson

All rights reserved. No part of this book may be reproduced of transmitted in any form or by any means, electronic or mechanical, including photocopying, recording or by any information storage and retrieval system without written permission of the publisher, except for inclusion of brief quotations in a review.

Printed in the United States of America

Library of Congress Control Number: 2013922141

ISBN-13: 978-1494329884

ISBN-10: 1494329883

Warning – Disclaimer

The purpose of this book is to educate and entertain. This book does not promise or guarantee that anyone following the ideas, tips, suggestions, techniques or strategies will be successful. The author, publisher and distributor(s) shall have neither liability nor responsibility to anyone with respect to any loss or damage caused, or alleged to be caused, directly or indirectly by the information contained in this book.

Recent Books By The Author

Product Management

- Product Manager Product Success: How to keep your product on track and make it become a success

- Communication Skills For Product Managers: The Communication Skills That Product Managers Need To Know How To Use In Order To Have A Successful Product

- Customer Lessons For Product Managers: Techniques For Product Managers To Better Understand What Their Customers Really Want

Public Speaking

- Secrets To Planning The Perfect Speech

- Secrets To Organizing The Perfect Speech: How to organize the best speech of your life!

- Secrets To Creating The Perfect Speech: How to create a speech that will make your message be remembered forever!

- How To Rehearse In Order To Give The Perfect Speech: How to effectively rehearse your next speech to that your message be remembered forever!

CIO Skills

- Managing Your CIO Career: Steps That CIOs Have To Take In Order To Have A Long And Successful Career

- CIO Communication Skills Secrets: Tips And Techniques For CIOs To Use In Order To Become Better Communicators

- How CIOs Can Make Innovation Happen: Tips And Techniques For CIOs To Use In Order To Make Innovation Happen In Their IT Department

IT Manager Skills

- IT Manager Budgeting Skills

- IT Manager Career Secrets: Tips And Techniques That IT Managers Can Use In Order To Have A Successful Career

- Secrets Of Effective Leadership For IT Managers : Tips And Techniques That IT Managers Can Use In Order To Develop Leadership Skills

Negotiating

- Preparing For Your Next Negotiation: What You Need To Do BEFORE A Negotiation Starts In Order To Get The Best Possible Deal

- How To Open Your Next Negotiation: How To Start A Negotiation In Order To Get The Best Possible Outcome

Note: See a complete list of books by Dr. Jim Anderson at the back of this book.

Acknowledgements

Any book like this one is the result of years of real-world work experience. In my over 25 years of working for 7 different firms, I have met countless fantastic people and I've been mentored by some truly exceptional ones. Although I've probably forgotten some of the people who made me the person that I am today, here is my attempt to finally give them the recognition that they so truly deserve:

- Thomas P. Anderson
- Art Puett
- Bobbi Marshall
- Bob Boggs

Dr. Jim Anderson

This book is dedicated to my wife Lori. None of this would have been possible without her love and support.

Thanks for the best 21 years of my life (so far)...!

Table Of Contents

TO GET WHAT YOU WANT, YOU HAVE TO KNOW HOW TO ARGUE ... 8

ABOUT THE AUTHOR 10

CHAPTER 1: NEGOTIATION DO'S & DON'TS FROM THE MASTER NEGOTIATORS 15

CHAPTER 2: POWER LOSS IN SALES NEGOTIATIONS 20

CHAPTER 3: HOW TO PLAY (& WIN) WHEN THERE'S ONLY ONE GAME IN TOWN 23

CHAPTER 4: HOW TO NEGOTIATE A RAISE 27

CHAPTER 5: GET YOUR ARMOR ON! 4 WAYS TO DEFEND YOUR PRICE DURING A SALES NEGOTIATION 31

CHAPTER 6: 2 "NEVER FAIL" SECRETS TO GETTING YOUR WAY IN A SALES NEGOTIATION 35

CHAPTER 7: HOW TO USE THE "PIVOT TECHNIQUE" TO DEFEND YOUR PRICE DURING A SALES NEGOTIATION 39

CHAPTER 8: WHY SALES NEGOTIATIONS ALWAYS SEEM TO BE A FAILURE EARLY ON 42

CHAPTER 9: SALES NEGOTIATORS NEED TO BE GOOD PRESSURE THINKERS 45

CHAPTER 10: YES, YOU CAN BUY NOW AND NEGOTIATE LATER – BUT BE CAREFUL… 49

CHAPTER 11: SALES NEGOTIATORS KNOW THAT IT'S OK TO NOT UNDERSTAND THINGS 53

CHAPTER 12: WHY IT'S OK FOR A SALES NEGOTIATOR TO BE WRONG 57

To Get What You Want, You Have To Know How To Argue

We all know how we want our next negotiation to end – with a good deal for us. However, what all too often we don't spend enough time on understanding is how important our ability to successfully argue our points will be in order to get to that desired deal.

So much of what goes on in a negotiation is about power. Who has it, who is losing it, who is gaining it, and why. You have the ability to control the balance of power in a negotiation through the force of your arguments if you know how.

Although no negotiation is just about price, it sure seems as though a great deal of our time and our negotiating energy is taken up by dealing with all of the issues surrounding both the price that we want and the price that we are willing to give. How your ability to argue is can have a significant impact on how good of a job you are going to be able to do in defending your price.

Negotiating is all about strategies and techniques. In order to get what you want out of your next negotiation you need to learn how to use the pivot technique as a part of your argument strategy in order to create the opportunity for you to get the deal that you want.

All too often we start to feel a great deal of pressure to make sure that we know everything about everything before the negotiations start. However, the good news is that recent discoveries have shown that you can still successfully win the arguments that naturally occur during a negotiation even if you don't know the answer to every possible question.

The world of negotiating can be confusing and challenging. This book has been created to act as your guide as you explore how to boost your ability to successful argue during a negotiation. By using the ideas and techniques outlined in this book you can take control of the negotiations during arguments and drive the discussions towards achieving the deal that you are looking for.

For more information on what it takes to be a great negotiator, check out my blog, The Accidental Negotiator, at:

www.TheAccidentalNegotiator.com

Good luck!

- Dr. Jim Anderson

About The Author

I must confess that I never set out to be a negotiator. When I went to school, I studied Computer Science and thought that I'd get a nice job programming and that would be that. Well, at least part of that plan worked out!

My first job was working for Boeing on their F/A-18 fighter jet program. I spent my days programming fighter jet software in assembly language and I loved it. The U.S. government decided to save some money and went looking for other countries to sell this plane to. This put me into an unfamiliar role: I started to negotiate with foreign military officials and I ended up having to participate in the negotiations for large international deals.

Time moved on and so did I. I found myself working for Siemens, the big German telecommunications company. They were making phone switches and selling them to the seven U.S. phone companies. The problem was that the switches were too complicated. When it came time to negotiate a deal with the customer, the sales teams struggled to create an effective negotiating strategy. I was called in to bridge the world between the product functionality and the business impacts as they related to the negotiations.

I've spent over 25 years working as a negotiator for both big companies and startups. This has given me an opportunity to learn what it takes to both plan and execute negotiations of all sizes. When it comes to negotiations, I've pretty much been there, done that.

I now live in Tampa Florida where I spend my time managing my consulting business, Blue Elephant Consulting, teaching college courses at the University of South Florida, and traveling to work with companies like yours to share the knowledge that I have about how to prepare for and execute successful negotiations.

I'm always available to answer questions and I can be reached at:

Dr. Jim Anderson
Blue Elephant Consulting
Email: jim@BlueElephantConsulting.com
Facebook: http://goo.gl/1TVoK
Web: **www.BlueElephantConsulting.com**

"Unforgettable communication skills that will set your ideas free..."

Create An Effective Negotiating Team At Your Company!

Dr. Jim Anderson is available to provide training and coaching on the topics that are the most important to people who have to negotiate: how can my team effectively prepare for and execute a successful negotiation that will get us what we both want and need?

Dr. Anderson believes that in order to both learn and remember what he says, audiences need to laugh. Each one of his speeches is full of fun and humor so that what he says "sticks" with everyone.

Dr. Anderson's Negotiating Training Includes:

1. How to plan for a negotiation: what information do you need and where can you find it?

2. What's the best way to explore how a deal can be created during a negotiation?

3. How can you bring a negotiation to a close without giving in to the other side?

Dr. Jim Anderson works with over 100 customers per year. To invite Dr. Anderson to work with you, contact him at:

Phone: 813-418-6970 or
Email: jim@BlueElephantConsulting.com

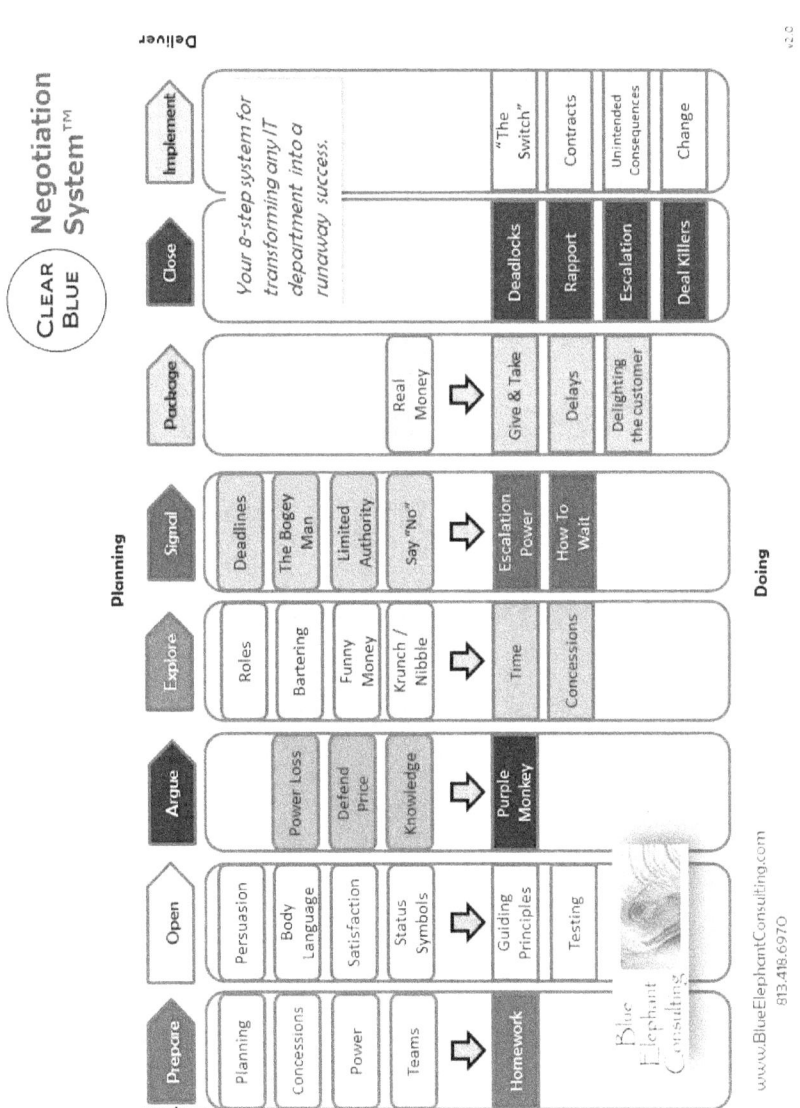

The **Clear Blue Negotiation System™** has been created to provide negotiators with a clear roadmap for how to manage a successful negotiation. This system shows negotiators what needs to be done and in what order to do it.

Chapter 1

Negotiation Do's & Don'ts From The Master Negotiators

Chapter 1: Negotiation Do's & Don'ts From The Master Negotiators

If only there was some book to read, some DVD to watch, or some class that you could take that would provide you with access to all of the secrets of those master negotiators whom we are always reading about. You know the ones, they negotiate the billion dollar business deal, the hostage negotiations, they settle the labor strikes, and they come up with solutions to lawsuits before they hit the courts. Just what are their secrets?

Bad news, there are no such courses, DVDs, or courses to take because of the nature of negotiating: it's not just a couple of key ideas, but rather a whole bunch of very small things that when taken together make a master negotiator.

However, there is no need to despair! The good folks over at the negotiating teaching company Karrass have been doing research into what makes a good negotiator for quite some time. Based on this they have been able to pull together a list of ten things that a master negotiator needs to be able to do.

What I'm hoping that you'll get from this list is the awareness that there is nothing earth shattering here. No great secrets are revealed. No hidden negotiating ninja secrets are being brought to the surface for the first time. Rather, a set of skills are being identified as being those skills that a master negotiator needs to have.

It's not that a master negotiator has just one of these skills that makes them so skillful. Rather it's the fact that they have ALL of these skills that makes them a master negotiator. Now there's something to think about! Here's the list, let's see how many of these negotiating skills you already have:

1. **Nothing Is Fixed:** Don't let the other side of the table try to intimidate you with "last & final" offers, firm fixed prices, or even "take it or leave it" statements. Remember – this is a negotiation and that means that everything is negotiable.

2. **Deeper Is Better For Both Sides:** Although you are negotiating directly with the person(s) on the other side of the table, you are really negotiating with their entire organization. This means that before your negotiating partner can agree to your terms, they are going to have to get buy-in from their organization. During your negotiations you need to cover all of the key details in enough depth that the other side will be able to thoroughly explain the deal internally.

3. **Got To Get Satisfaction:** Forget win-lose, win-win, etc. Negotiating is all about making sure that both sides come away feeling satisfied with the outcome. Although it's easy to focus on the stated negotiation issues, be sure to look for other "hidden" issues that are also important to the other side. Addressing these issues will boost satisfaction and increase the probability of reaching an agreement.

4. **These Boots Are Made For Walking:** One of the most powerful negotiating techniques is also one of the most difficult to do – leave & walk out. This by itself would kill a negotiation, so you also have to master the other half of this skill – you need to know when to return later on.

5. **Conflict Is King:** The very reason that you are negotiating is because there are differences between both sides. Differences mean that there will be conflicts. You need to be able to deal with conflict. If you have an overpowering need to be liked, then you will end up giving too much away during the negotiation just to be

reassured that the other side likes you in the end.

6. **Too Much:** In any negotiation, you can screw up. You can end up asking the other side for more than they are willing / able to give. When you realize that you've done this is the time for you to take a step back and tell the other side that you are willing to renegotiate. No matter what, make sure that you show empathy for the other side's situation.

7. **No Such Thing As Too Much Education:** You will never know everything that there is to know about negotiation. There are so many small tricks & techniques that it will take you a lifetime to master even some of them. This means that you always need to be reading and studying in order to boost your knowledge of negotiating strategy & tactics.

8. **Aim High:** Where you end up in a negotiation has a great deal to do with where you set your target. If you aim high, then you will be prepared to take the negotiating risks that go with higher goals. Lofty goals don't come easily so you are going to have to be willing to work hard and to take your time.

9. **Be Testy:** Since you can never completely know what the other side of the table is thinking, you need to always be testing him / her. You just might surprise yourself when the other side gives in to one of your demands. Once again, this type of testing requires that you take your time and be very, very patient.

10. **Take Your Team To School:** Negotiating is often a team sport and you want your team to be in the best shape possible. You need to make sure that your team has been trained to negotiate the way that you want them to. This is the one area that investing in quality training

(just like the training offered by Blue Elephant Consulting) can really pay dividends.

Chapter 2

Power Loss In Sales Negotiations

Chapter 2: Power Loss In Sales Negotiations

The single most important factor in determining how a negotiation is going to turn out centers on a single question: **who has the most power**? The big problem that most of us have is that we don't think that we have enough of it. Turns out, we're generally wrong about this...

The Secret Of Negotiating Power

What is power in a sales negotiation? Simple – it's the ability of one side of the table to **control** both the resources that are available to the other side as well as the benefits that they can get.

At all times during a sales negotiation it is your responsibility to be looking for ways to **build up your power base** while at the same time working to prevent the other side of the table from gaining leverage over you (and thereby causing you to experience power loss).

Where Does Your Power Come From?

All too often when I'm talking with sales negotiators, they'll tell me that they don't feel as though they have enough negotiating power to be successful in an upcoming bargaining session. When we talk a bit more, it quickly becomes apparent that they are only seeing half the story. Specifically, they are only thinking about "**positive power**".

Positive negotiating power comes from all of the things that put you in a **good position to negotiate**. Having plenty of time to make a deal, having attractive alternatives, having plenty of funding, etc. – these are all sources of positive power for you.

What my clients always seem to overlook is that they also have "**negative power**" working for them. Negative negotiating power comes from **limitations and restrictions** that the other side of the table is working under. These can include the need to reach a deal quickly, not having a good alternative to dealing with you, or even limited availability of funds.

Final Thoughts

The power that you have during a sales negotiation isn't something that sits on the table next to you. Instead, it's more like a **feeling of confidence** that you have when you sit down at the table.

Not only do you have the easily recognizable sources of **positive power** working for you, you also have the hidden sources of **negative power** on your side also. If you can learn to spot both of these power sources before you enter into your next negotiation, then you will be able to close better deals and close them quicker.

Chapter 3

How To Play (& Win) When There's Only One Game In Town

Chapter 3: How To Play (& Win) When There's Only One Game In Town

Having a single supplier for something that you want is the best thing in the world. "What?" you say, they've got me over a barrel and they can dictate any price or any conditions on a deal that they want because I have **no other alternative**.

Well, ok, that's one way to look at it if you want to be all negative and such. However, there's a different way to see things and when you look at the situation this way you'll see that it's you who has them over a barrel. Let me explain.

How'd You Get Into This Situation?

When we are starting a project, creating a new product, or we just find something that we just HAVE TO have, we can suddenly discover a big BLAM! This occurs when there is some component of our plan that is **controlled by someone else**. When that thing is the ONE thing that we must have to make our plan succeed then that vendor is a sole supplier to us. Sure looks like we're in a bind here.

Options, Options, Options

The first thing that you need to realize is that you are only in a pickle **if you think that you are**. This type of situation calls for some problem solving. What's the one thing that all sales negotiators know: it's all about power, the more that you have, the better the outcome of the sales negotiation will be for you. Feeling powerless is not a good way to start any negotiating relationship!

You always have what I like to refer to as the **"nuclear option"**. What this means is that if you can't reach an agreement with the person who has control over the one thing that you need, then you can always chose option B: "make" your own.

In business this could mean that you'd set up a factory to make **your own version** of whatever parts the supplier is controlling. In your personal life, if the seller of the house that you just must have won't sell to you at a reasonable price, then you can always go out and build your own house that looks just like his.

Build Your Own Competition

Although there may not be other sources for the thing that you want, another option that you can bring to the table is to **create competition** between the supplier and himself. You've got to realize that he's got both short term and long term goals.

You've actually got a lot of control over the deal. You can control how much you are willing to buy, when you'll take delivery of it, and (most importantly) when you'll pay and in what amounts you'll pay. Both pre-paying and delaying payments can have a significant impact on the other side's tax situation, etc. and **you hold the keys** to when this will happen.

Creating A Second Source

Negotiation tactics can be used **to give you more negotiating power** in a single supplier situation like this. One such tactic is to actively create a second supplier. Even if such a supplier does not currently exist, you can approach a potential firm and find out if the offer of some or all of your business would motivate them to become a supplier of the needed item.

If you are able to convince them to do this, then you will have created **true competition**. However, you will need to make sure that you don't get locked into this second supplier as your only source of the item!

What This All Means For You

The worst thing in the world that can happen to a sales negotiator is that you find yourself in a negotiation where you have **no negotiating power**. In a situation like this you'll end up just having to agree to whatever the other side proposes.

However, you should realize that no negotiation ever has to be like this. Instead, you have to realize that **you always have options**. Even in a situation where you need to have something that someone else controls, you still have options. You can always choose to build your own option, you can cause the other side to compete with themselves, or you can go out and work with another supplier to create true competition.

No matter how you choose to handle it, you will have taken some of the power that seemed to all start on the other side of the table and then **you were able to bring it over to your side**. Now doesn't that make you happier?

Chapter 4

How To Negotiate A Raise

Chapter 4: How To Negotiate A Raise

Even negotiators need to get paid. This might be a good time to have a talk about one of your most important types of negotiations: **asking for a raise**. Wait a minute: did I see you just grimace? Did you turn away? Why the reaction – it's your paycheck after all, shouldn't you be taking charge of how much you make?

If you are counting on getting a big raise this year, you might want to think again. The folks over at Hewitt Associates are saying that raises this year are going to be running **at about 3% or so** – nothing to write home about.

What you are going to want to do is to find a way to get in the running to get your hands on some of your company's **incentive pay**. The folks at Hewitt are saying that the budgets for incentive pay are running at about 7% or so – clearly there's more money to be had in this bucket.

A Little Strategy Goes A Long Way

If you are going to have a chance to be successful in getting more money out of your employer, you're going to have to **come up with a plan** in order to make it happen. Robert Moskowitz has spent some time studying what needs to be done and he's come up with some suggestions for us. Here's what he thinks that we need to do:

- **Create A Price Tag For Yourself:** Just how much are you worth in today's market? This is a critical piece of information that you need to know. It may require a bit of research on your part: talking with head hunters, reading online and print ads for similar positions, and generally asking around within your network. With a little luck you'll find out that you are being underpaid!

- **Boost Your Value:** Every company has a different set of skills and responsibilities that they view as being the most valuable. You need to take a step back and understand what is the most important to your company: is it financial skills? Marketing skills? Selling skills? Once you know what is the most valued, you need to take steps to increase your value in these areas.

- **Get Your Head In The Game:** The odds of you getting fired for asking for a raise are so slim that you need to not worry about it. Increase your feeling of self-confidence by picturing yourself as being successful and don't worry about any pushback that you might get.

- **See Into The Future:** and identify what objections your boss might bring up. Make sure that when you make your request for more money you touch on these points and offer solutions to them before they are bought up.

Good Tactics Can Make All The Difference

Even before you go into your boss' office to request a raise, there are a number of things that you can do in order to **improve your odds of success**. Here are a few of them:

- **It's All About Performance:** You need to spend some time creating a list of why you should get more money. Weak reasons like the length of time since you got your last raise won't do the trick – it's got to be based on bottom line results.

- **Documents Count:** having physical proof that you have had superior job performance can be critical to making your case. This of course means that you need to have been keeping a file that shows what you've accomplished throughout the past year.

- **Practice, Practice, Practice:** In order to prepare yourself for the big event, spend the week before you make your request practicing with yourself. This will help you to get your words straight and will allow you to prepare to deal with most likely feedback that you should expect.

What All Of This Means For You

Coming out of the global recession, we are all probably **not being paid what we are worth**. It's time to ask for either a raise or at least a bonus.

As scary as the prospect of asking for a raise may be, there are things that you can do in order **to boost your odds**. Keep in mind that it's your value to the company and your past performance that will boost your odds of getting more money in your paycheck.

It is possible to ask for a raise and get it. It just takes a bit of preparation and **some good negotiating skills**…!

Chapter 5

Get Your Armor On! 4 Ways To Defend Your Price During A Sales Negotiation

Chapter 5: Get Your Armor On! 4 Ways To Defend Your Price During A Sales Negotiation

Much has been written (some of it by me) about what a sales negotiator can do when the other side of the table has set a fixed price and just won't budge. We've come up with all sorts of ways to turn a fixed price into not such a fixed price. This time out, **let's switch sides** and spend some time talking about what you can do to defend your price when you are the seller – how do you counter all of those clever tactics that the other side has?

It's Not All About The Price

When you are trying to sell something to the other side, clearly both of you **have different goals**. You are trying to get the highest price for your product while at the same time the other side is trying to get the lowest price. Something's got to give.

The other side will probably be **hammering you on price**. A common tactic is to point out that they can go to other suppliers and get the same product for a lower price. They want you to give in and lower your price.

If you hear this often enough, you might actually start to believe it – don't! Instead you need to realize that what you are offering **is unique in some way**. Maybe it's how you deliver the product, how you stand behind it, or any one of a number of different factors. These make your offering both unique and valuable. Don't give in!

Stop The Brainwashing Immediately!

When you are involved in a sales negotiation, you enter a strange little world. In this alternate universe how you see what you are trying to sell to the other side is shaped not by what you think about it, not by what all of your other customers have told you, but rather by **what the other side is telling you about it right now**.

This means that if they tell you something over and over again, there is a good chance that what they are saying will soon **shape your view of your product**. If they say that there is nothing special about your product and that the price that you are charging is too high, then you'll start to believe them after a while.

You need to make sure that this doesn't occur. There are lots of ways to do this. One of my favorite ways is to bring a folder along with me to the sales negotiation which contains clippings and notes on why my product is so valuable. During breaks I'll leaf through this folder quickly **just to remind myself** why my product is not only the best product available, but also why it is worth the price that I am charging for it.

Make The Other Side Want To Date You

There are lots of ways to treat the other side of the table during a negotiation and I've seen all of it done at some time or another. Over and over again what has worked the best is when you show the other side that **you appreciate them and want to do business with them**.

Sure there are lot of "tough guy" approaches that you can take ("I don't need this sale"), but I've found that you're going to end up making more concessions when you take this path. Play it straight, show the other side some love and **you'll make a better deal every time**.

Defend Your Price By Bringing Up The Total Cost

Often when we are selling a "thing" or a service, the negotiations can come down to focusing on the price of the "thing". As the selling side of the table, you need to steer the discussion to consider **the total cost of the "thing"**.

This means that you need to get the other side of the table to sit back and **consider the entire ecosystem** that your product will be used in. Things like installation, maintenance, replacement, reliability, and servicing need to be included in the consideration. If you are careful to include the right components, then you can easily justify your price.

What All Of This Means For You

When you are on the selling side in a sales negotiation, you need to understand that the other side will be doing everything in their power to try to get you to **lower your price**. Don't do it!

There are a number of different ways that you can defend the price that you are offering your product or service at. **Expanding the negotiation** and making sure that it doesn't just focus on price will allow you to justify the price that you are asking.

In the end, your ability to defend your price plays two roles. It will, of course, determine how successful you will be as a sales negotiator and it will also **raise the value of the product that you are selling** in the buyer's eyes.

Chapter 6

2 "Never Fail" Secrets To Getting Your Way In A Sales Negotiation

Chapter 6: 2 "Never Fail" Secrets To Getting Your Way In A Sales Negotiation

Hey, did you read any of those Harry Potter books (or at least see one of the movies?) If you did, then you probably got drawn into **the world of magic and wizards** that the books are all about. It sure seems as though in these stories that there is a magic portion or a curse to do just about anything. The stories are fiction but it turns out that sales negotiators do have some real magic that they can use to get what they want during a negotiation…

The Power Of The Word "No"

For some odd reason in Western cultures there seems to be **a social stigma** associated with saying the word "no" to someone – even when we're in the middle of a sales negotiation. If you want to be successful, you're going to have to learn to get over this hang up.

I'm not talking about just saying "no" and then turning your back to the other side of the table. Instead, I'm going to suggest **a two-part "no" strategy**. The first part, naturally, consists of you saying "no". The second part is where you take the time to explain to the other side of the table WHY you said no. The goal here is to explain your reasoning in a clear and logical fashion.

One of the reasons that so many of us really dislike saying (or sticking with) a "no" is because we think that it's going to make the other side of the table **feel bad**. What's interesting about this is that more often than not, we're wrong about this.

Getting a "no" from us might be exactly what the other side of the table wants. It **closes the door** on this part of the negotiation and so they can move on to the next part. If asked by their bosses, they can at least say that they asked and we said "no".

In the world of negotiating, just about everyone agrees that **the Japanese are the best at saying "no"** . They have a way of saying it in such a way that you don't feel bad when you hear it: "yes, but …" or "no, maybe…".

Give Them An Opportunity To Vent

Just how do you think your response of a "no" is going to make the other side of the table feel? **Sad? Angry? You bet!** When they are feeling this way they are going to want to vent, let off some steam. If you are wise, you'll go ahead and let them do this.

The reasoning behind this strategy is subtle, but complex. By allowing the other side to go on a rant, you are deliberately **not restricting their actions**. If you tried to do this they just might go postal and storm out of the negotiations. By allowing them to do some yelling, you are providing them with a safe way to work through their frustrations.

Another point that you should keep in mind is that when the other side is venting, they may actually be **showing off** for the rest of their team. Remember that when the sales negotiations are done, they are going to have to report to their bosses who will ask if they did everything that they could in order to get the best deal possible. Reports of their tirade may serve to convince their internal audience that they did a good job.

What All Of This Means For You

Forget the magic that Harry Potter is able to call upon, today's sales negotiators need to find **some practical magic**. The good news is that there seems to be plenty of it around for us to use.

The simple word "no" can be the one word that allows you to **get what you want** during your next sales negotiation. You just need to find the courage to say it and stick with it. Once you've said it, you'll need to give the other side of the table a chance to work out their frustration.

If you can do both of these things, then you'll be that much closer to **striking a good deal** during your next negotiation. Who can say "no" to that?

Chapter 7

How To Use The "Pivot Technique" To Defend Your Price During A Sales Negotiation

Chapter 7: How To Use The "Pivot Technique" To Defend Your Price During A Sales Negotiation

I just love Ferris wheels. They are generally huge, have the ability to take you way up into the sky and then always bring you safely back down to earth. If you've ever taken the time to look at how a Ferris wheel is built, then you already know about one of the **key negotiating techniques** that top sales negotiators use when they need to defend a price…

How Ferris Wheels Are Like Sales Negotiating

Many sales negotiations get hung up and fall apart when the discussion finally gets around to **the issue of price**. The reason for this is pretty simple: one side of the table wants a lower price and the other side either doesn't want to or can't lower it. End of discussion – both sides shake hands and walk away without a deal.

It turns out that things don't have to end this way. The **"pivot technique"** is one way that experienced sales negotiators have found to meet this issue head on and not derail the negotiations. One way to mentally picture the pivot technique in action is to think of a Ferris wheel with a center hub and passenger holding cars (gondolas) distributed in a circle around the hub.

The Pivot Technique In Action

Think of the price of your product or service as being **the hub of a Ferris wheel** – it's both fixed and unmoving. However, a Ferris wheel with just a hub is no fun at all. That's why it has gondolas to carry passengers. In the pivot technique these gondolas represent other negotiating points that you can use to make sure that the negotiations continue even when you have a fixed hub.

Although this may seem obvious, during the heat of a negotiation it's not – **you don't focus on the hub**, you spend your time talking about the gondolas. There are a lot of different ways to do this: the number of gondolas and just exactly what is in them is completely up to you.

Don't get me wrong: neither you nor the other side is going to forget that this is all being held together by **an immovable hub**. However, as the number of gondolas increases and their contents become more desirable, the hub will cease to become as much of a significant issue.

What All Of This Means For You

A sales negotiation that falls apart because of price is **a tragedy that didn't need to happen**. Yes, price is important to both sides; however, the total value of the deal is much more important.

The pivot technique is a tool that experienced negotiators use to get around the problem of having to negotiate with **a price that can't be lowered**. By adding additional points to negotiate to the table, we have the ability to build a complete package to be negotiated and this makes the price only a single component of a much bigger deal.

There are no **silver bullets** in sales negotiations. However, the pivot technique is a powerful tool that can help you avoid having your next sales negotiation come to an end because you couldn't change your price.

Chapter 8

Why Sales Negotiations Always Seem To Be A Failure Early On

Chapter 8: Why Sales Negotiations Always Seem To Be A Failure Early On

I often like to think of a sales negotiation as being **very similar to a dance**. The first few moves are very well known and are recognized by both sides. However, very quickly things can get out of control. Neither partner recognizes what the other partner is doing and toes start to get stepped on. Does it always have to go this way?

The Beginning Of Bargaining

Unfortunately I believe that the answer is "yes". Ever sales negotiation seems to **follow a fairly predictable course**. We always seem to start out on the right footing – doesn't every negotiation start with pleasant introductions?

It's what happens after the introductions that the expert negotiators focus on the most. They realize that **the next step is when the real bargaining starts**.

Once upon a time I took a business course on **"organizational behavior"**. Although that was a long time ago, I can still remember the phases that people go through when you throw them together as a part of a team: forming, storming, conforming, and norming. After I took this course I can remember being amazed when I observed that in real life these really are the steps that teams go through.

The same can be said of sales negotiations – **they too seem to follow a standard path**...

Why Can't We All Just Get Along...?

Why does it have to be this way? Sales negotiations always seem to quickly descend into hostility and verbal sparring. For the sensitive negotiator this can quickly appear to be **movement in the wrong direction**.

We need to understand why this happens. One of the key reasons is that at the start of a negotiation both sides of the table are **as far apart as they are ever going to be**.

We all enter a negotiation with a starting position (what we want) that may **appear to be unrealistic to the other side**. This is going to make the other side think that the possibility of reaching an agreement with us may be out of the question.

We all react to this situation in the same way. We attack the other side's position and **force them to defend themselves**. We force them and they force us to take different postures in order to justify where they are coming from.

What All Of This Means For You

Every sales negotiation **has its ugly parts**. Most often right after the negotiations start, things appear to head off into the wrong direction.

Experienced sales negotiators realize that this is a normal part of every negotiation. Since both sides start so far apart, **conflict and disagreement are to be expected**.

The key is to realize that **this is only one part of a much larger negotiation**. If you can make it through this part, then things will get better. Remember, things always seem the darkest just before the dawn…

Chapter 9

Sales Negotiators Need To Be Good Pressure Thinkers

Chapter 9: Sales Negotiators Need To Be Good Pressure Thinkers

Let's face it: a sales negotiation is **a high-pressure situation**. With all that is expected of you, thinking clearly can be a challenge even for the best of us. That's why the best sales negotiators have developed a whole series of techniques that provided them with the time that they need to do a good job of thinking under pressure…

It Takes A Village To Think Under Pressure

As sales negotiators, **we think pretty highly of ourselves**. When it comes to making decisions under pressure, however, we're no better than the next guy. That's why when we have the option; we should never go it alone.

Instead, when we attend a sales negotiation we should always bring along someone else from our team, and more if we can get away with it. The thinking here is pretty simple. By having multiple people on your team, you'll have **an excuse for everything to take longer**. You'll need to discuss things, come to a consensus, look things up, etc.

All of these activities take time. This is time that you can use to think about the current negotiating situation and make decisions about what you want to do next. It does seem to slow down the overall negotiations; however, this extra time is exactly what you need in order to be able to make good decisions under pressure.

It's Recess Time (Again)!

Nobody ever said that you needed to sit down at the negotiating table and not get up again until you've reached a deal with the other side. In fact, you are probably **not going to be happy** with the deal that you agree to if you negotiate this way.

Instead, a better way of doing things is to **take frequent breaks** throughout the negotiations. Every time you take a break, use the time to go over your notes, think about how you want to respond to what has been said by the other side, and perhaps even adjust your strategy.

It's my opinion that **you can't take too many breaks** during a negotiation. If the other side really wants to strike a deal with you, they'll have to go along with all of your break requests. The more time that you have to think, the better the final deal that you'll be able reach.

The Long Pause

Rare is the sales negotiation that can be completed in a single day. This **opens an opportunity** for you to buy yourself more time to make better decisions.

Take a look at the calendar before the negotiation starts. Are there any natural breaks that are going to occur during the negotiations: a meal, the end of the day, a weekend, a holiday, etc.? Once you've identified such a break, **use it to your advantage**.

Suggest an agenda that will result in the other side using the available time to lay out their position. You want them to **use up all of the available time**. Feel free to ask questions about the material that they are presenting in order to ensure that there is no time left over.

When you reach the natural breaking point, suggest that the break be taken and that you'll respond to what has been presented after the break. By doing this you ensure that you'll have **the maximum amount of time** to consider what the other side has presented and you'll be able to make your best decisions – not under pressure!

What All Of This Means For You

Top sales negotiators know that in order to get the best deal possible, they are going to have to **do a good job of thinking under pressure**. The trick to doing this well is to set things up so that you have the time that you need to make good decisions.

In order to **provide yourself with the time that you'll need**, make sure that you bring people with you to your next negotiation. Once there, don't be afraid to take many breaks – these allow you time to think and change your strategy. Finally, schedule the negotiation so that you have the maximum amount of time after the other side has presented their position before you have to respond to it.

By allowing yourself enough time to think about what your next move is going to be, no matter how much pressure you are under, you will always come out of a negotiation **in a better position**. The key to long-term negotiating success is to find ways to provide yourself with enough time to make the correct decisions. Now you know how to do this!

Chapter 10

Yes, You Can Buy Now And Negotiate Later – But Be Careful...

Chapter 10: Yes, You Can Buy Now And Negotiate Later – But Be Careful…

How do you feel about negotiating? If you really don't like to do it, then I've got a great option for you: just go ahead and buy something and then **worry about doing the negotiating later on**. Wait you say, is this even possible? The answer is yes, but you might want to think twice before you do it…

The Idea Behind Negotiating Later On

The very idea of agreeing to make a purchase and then putting the negotiating off until later on **seems crazy**, doesn't it? Under normal circumstances, I'd agree with you; however, not all circumstances that we find ourselves in are what we'd call "normal"…

An obvious case in point would be a situation in which you have **very limited time** to find a solution to a problem. If your car breaks down on the highway, then the first tow truck that comes along is the one that you'll be willing to purchase towing services from with basically no negotiation. After you've been towed to a gas station, that's when the real negotiating will probably start.

The disadvantage of handling deal making this way can be significant. Once you've told the other side of the table that you're going to buy from them, you're basically **locked in**. This means that a great deal of the power in the eventual negotiations has transferred from you to the other side.

Additionally, the other side is in the driver's seat when it comes to **setting a final price** for the item that you've purchased. Under the wrong circumstances, you may end up paying a much higher price than the thing that you bought was worth.

Why Putting Off Negotiating Might Be A Good Idea — Sometimes

So clearly there are some risks to deferring the process of negotiating a deal. However, at the same time there are a number of reasons that **you might want to consider this approach** to resolving an issue.

Many tasks that we are looking to have others complete for us are complex. The ability to fully evaluate the other side of the table's ability to do the work **can be prohibitive**. Simply awarding them the job and then evaluating their work once they're done can be a clever way of determining their skill level.

Using the other side of the table's known history of deal making can provide you with **the confidence to move faster**. If you need to have the work done and you believe that you can trust the other side to strike a fair deal, then buying before you negotiate can provide you with the advantage of speed.

Not all jobs can be fully estimated before the work is started. For this type of work, you're going to have to select your partner and have the work commence before you can determine **just exactly how large the deal is**. Situations like this are perfect for using a "not to exceed" clause in order to make sure that you are not taken advantage of.

What All Of This Means For You

It turns out that it is possible to **turn the standard negotiating model on its head** and buy something first, and then agree to negotiate later on. This is a unique way of going about getting what you want right now!

Setting up a deal this way comes with **a series of risks**. The most important of these risks is that you are now locked into using a single vendor – they've got you. However, this approach can be used when you simply don't have any time to go through the full negotiating process.

The most important thing is to know is **who you are dealing with**. When you know the other side of the table, then you are able to make a judgment call about whether the risk is worth the reward. Under the right circumstances, this can be the right way to quickly solve a problem.

Chapter 11

Sales Negotiators Know That It's Ok To Not Understand Things

Chapter 11: Sales Negotiators Know That It's Ok To Not Understand Things

One of the great myths of sales negotiating is that **you always have to know everything about everything**. It turns out that even the great negotiators can't do this.

There are a whole bunch of reasons why, but the important fact is that it's not possible to always be on top of everything. It's what you do when you find yourself in this situation where you don't know everything that will distinguish you from other negotiators.

Why You Are Not Perfect

You aren't perfect – so get over it. Even in the best of circumstances a negotiation is **a fast-paced affair**.

During a negotiation we are trying to impress the other people on our team with how good of a negotiator we are. At the same time, we'd like to be able to impress the other side with how sharp and on the ball we are. The problem is that we fall off of that ball quite often.

Specifically what happens is that we get hit with a tidal wave of information as a negotiation progresses. The other side starts to throw facts, statistics, requirements, and demands at us very quickly. Trying to keep track of all that is being discussed **can overwhelm** even the sharpest negotiator.

Keep in mind that you are also under a great deal of pressure when you are part of a negotiation. There is generally a great deal riding on your ability to reach a deal that will allow your company to achieve great things. This pressure combined with lots of confusing information being thrown at you serves to **leave you feeling lost and confused**.

What You Need To Do When You Get Lost During A Negotiation

Becoming lost at some point during a sales negotiation is actually a fairly common occurrence – it happens to all of us at some time. When it happens to you, you'll need to remember the most important rule: **don't panic!**

Instead, realize what is happening – too much information, too much pressure, too little time to process it all. The first thing that you need to do is to **apply the brakes** to the negotiation. If you let it keep going on while you aren't following along, then you'll just end up getting more and more lost.

You need to speak up. Tell the other side that you don't understand what's been said and that you'd like them to back up and review where things currently stand. No, they aren't going to be terribly happy about this, but they'd do it – they don't have any other choice.

Many times what you'll discover when you do this is that the other side is not really sure where things stand either. They won't be able to back up because **they can't remember everything that they've said**. When this is discovered, you'll have a chance to reset the negotiations. You get to pick where things stand and the negotiations can start from there. You'll be in charge and you won't be lost anymore...!

What All Of This Means For You

I've got good news for you: **you don't have to be perfect** in order to be a very effective sales negotiator. What this means is that you can become lost during a sales negotiation and still end up with a good deal.

The reasons that we can get lost during a negotiation are many and varied. The most common one is that the other side **wanted us to become lost** and they buried us under a mountain of information that we just haven't been able to process. That's why it's always ok for us to say that we're confused and have the other side repeat themselves.

The burden of making sure that we understand what is being discussed really **falls on the other side of the table**. The only way that we can make a mistake is if we don't speak up when we find that we are lost. Have the courage to speak your mind and ask for clarification and you'll find your way home and be able to reach deals that you'll be proud of.

Chapter 12

Why It's Ok For A Sales Negotiator To Be Wrong

Chapter 12: Why It's Ok For A Sales Negotiator To Be Wrong

When you become the best sales negotiator in the world **you'll be right all the time**. However, since you're not there yet, you should expect to be wrong – not all the time, but at least some of the time. There are a lot of different ways to handle this, what's the right way?

Why You'll Be Wrong

Wait a minute, if you are a good negotiator then why would you still be making mistakes? I mean, if you take the time to prepare for the negotiation, understand the other side of the table and what they are hoping to get out of the negotiation, and are up on your negotiating tactics, then there's **no way** that you can end up making mistakes, right?

Wrong. At the end of the day we're all human and that means that we're going to end up making mistakes. Negotiations are high-pressure communication sessions in which a great deal of information can flow back and forth over the table in a very short time. Your position and the other side's position can change in a heartbeat and keeping up with it all can be **too much** for even the best of us.

At any point in time during a negotiation you may find that you've made a concession that you should not have. Or perhaps you'll discover that some of the information that you presented in order to support one of your points was flawed in some way that the other side was able to point out to you. No matter the cause, the end result is the same – **you find yourself being wrong**.

What You Can Do When You Are Wrong

Unless you've successfully built yourself a time machine that you can step into whenever something like this happens, **once you're wrong, you're wrong**. This means that you're going to have to either ignore it or take some action.

The incorrect thing to do, in most cases, is to **ignore it**. If you've given something away, made a concession that you should not have, or if you've said something that you wish that you could take back, then you need to undo it. This means that you tell the other side that you've made a mistake. You own up to your error.

A negotiation is not like carving a stone – you can **undo things** that have already been done. What's even better is that you have options: you can undo things or you can ask the other side of the table to help you undo it.

No matter what, **a deal requires both sides to come to agreement**. If you are not happy about something that you've done, than this is not going to happen. Therefore, if you need to change something that has already been done just go ahead and do it. Yes, the other side is not going to be happy about this because it is going to delay the negotiations, but that's ok. Speaking up and correcting an error is how you are going to be able to reach an agreement that you'll feel comfortable living with.

What All Of This Means For You

Nobody is perfect and negotiators are no different than everyone else. This means that **we're going to be wrong some of the time**. It's what we do when we discover that we're wrong that separates the adequate negotiators from the great ones.

The reason that we **make mistakes** during a negotiation are many and varied. It's a high-pressure, fast moving environment and so the possibility that we'll do or say something that we don't mean to is very real.

When we make a mistake, the best thing for us to do is to speak up. Tell the other side that you've done or said something that you didn't mean and "take it back". A negotiation is not set in stone, you can hit rewind at any time. The other side might not be pleased, but you will feel much better for doing it.

As with all such things in life, being wrong during a sales negotiation is going to happen to all of us at probably more times than we care to admit. Realizing that it has happened is the first step to fixing the situation. Having **the courage to correct it** is the key to ending up with a successful deal in the end.

It's from the forge of failure that the steel of success is formed.

Hard Work Does Not Guarantee Success, But Success Does Not Happen Without Hard Work.

- Dr. Jim Anderson

Create An Effective Negotiating Team At Your Company!

Dr. Jim Anderson is available to provide training and coaching on the topics that are the most important to people who have to negotiate: how can my team effectively prepare for and execute a successful negotiation that will get us what we both want and need?

Dr. Anderson believes that in order to both learn and remember what he says, audiences need to laugh. Each one of his speeches is full of fun and humor so that what he says "sticks" with everyone.

Dr. Anderson's Negotiating Training Includes:

1. How to plan for a negotiation: what information do you need and where can you find it?

2. What's the best way to explore how a deal can be created during a negotiation?

3. How can you bring a negotiation to a close without giving in to the other side?

Dr. Jim Anderson works with over 100 customers per year. To invite Dr. Anderson to work with you, contact him at:

Phone: 813-418-6970 or
Email: jim@BlueElephantConsulting.com

Photo Credits:

Cover - By: Adam Arroyo
http://www.flickr.com/photos/nouqraz/

Chapter 1 - By: Brian Garrett
http://www.flickr.com/photos/28122162@N04/

Chapter 2 - By: Official U.S. Navy Page
http://www.flickr.com/photos/usnavy/

Chapter 3 - By: jdurham
http://www.morguefile.com/creative/jdurham

Chapter 4 - By: Penywise
http://www.morguefile.com/creative/Penywise

Chapter 5 - By: earl53
http://www.morguefile.com/creative/earl53

Chapter 6 - By: Nathan Gibbs
http://www.flickr.com/photos/nathangibbs/

Chapter 7 - By: Martin Abegglen
http://www.flickr.com/photos/twicepix/

Chapter 8 - By: Kim Hill
http://www.flickr.com/photos/karsund/

Chapter 9 - By: ian munroe
http://www.flickr.com/photos/ian_munroe/

Chapter 10 - By: Simon Webster
http://www.flickr.com/photos/12495774@N02/

Chapter 11 - By: The Tire Zoo
http://www.flickr.com/photos/new_and_used_tires/

Chapter 12 - By: AndyCunningham
http://www.flickr.com/photos/cunaldo/

Other Books By The Author

Product Management

- How To Have A Successful Product Manager Career: The Things That You Need To Be Doing TODAY In Order To Have A Successful Product Manager Career

- Product Manager Product Success: How to keep your product on track and make it become a success

- Communication Skills For Product Managers: The Communication Skills That Product Managers Need To Know How To Use In Order To Have A Successful Product

- Customer Lessons For Product Managers: Techniques For Product Managers To Better Understand What Their Customers Really Want

Public Speaking

- Secrets To Planning The Perfect Speech

- Secrets To Organizing The Perfect Speech: How to organize the best speech of your life!

- Secrets To Creating The Perfect Speech: How to create a speech that will make your message be remembered forever!

- How To Rehearse In Order To Give The Perfect Speech: How to effectively rehearse your next speech to that your message be remembered forever!

CIO Skills

- CIO Business Skills: How CIOs can work effectively with the rest of the company!

- Managing Your CIO Career: Steps That CIOs Have To Take In Order To Have A Long And Successful Career

- CIO Communication Skills Secrets: Tips And Techniques For CIOs To Use In Order To Become Better Communicators

- How CIOs Can Make Innovation Happen: Tips And Techniques For CIOs To Use In Order To Make Innovation Happen In Their IT Department

IT Manager Skills

- IT Manager Budgeting Skills

- IT Manager Career Secrets: Tips And Techniques That IT Managers Can Use In Order To Have A Successful Career

Negotiating

- Preparing For Your Next Negotiation: What You Need To Do BEFORE A Negotiation Starts In Order To Get The Best Possible Deal

- How To Open Your Next Negotiation: How To Start A Negotiation In Order To Get The Best Possible Outcome

- Learn How To Argue In Your Next Negotiation: How To Develop The Skill Of Effective Arguing In A Negotiation In Order To Get The Best Possible Outcome

Miscellaneous

- Power Distribution Unit (PDU) Secrets: What Everyone Who Works In A Data Center Needs To Know!

- Making The Jump: How To Land Your Dream Job When You Get Out Of College!

How To Develop The Skill Of Effective Arguing In A Negotiation In Order To Get The Best Possible Outcome

> This book has been written with one goal in mind – to show you how to successfully argue in your next negotiation. It's not easy being a negotiator and so we're going to show you how to successfully argue with the other side in order to get the deal that you want!
>
> **Let's Make Your Negotiation A Success!**

What You'll Find Inside:

- **POWER LOSS IN SALES NEGOTIATIONS**

- **HOW TO PLAY (& WIN) WHEN THERE'S ONLY ONE GAME IN TOWN**

- **GET YOUR ARMOR ON! 4 WAYS TO DEFEND YOUR PRICE DURING A SALES NEGOTIATION**

- **WHY IT'S OK FOR A SALES NEGOTIATOR TO BE WRONG**

Dr. Jim Anderson brings his 25 years of real-world experience to this book. He's been a negotiator at some of the world's largest firms. He's going to show you what you need to do (and not do!) in order to get the best deal out of your next negotiation!

www.ingramcontent.com/pod-product-compliance
Lightning Source LLC
Chambersburg PA
CBHW071807170526
45167CB00003B/1205